THE OPEN AGILE ADOPTION HANDBOOK

THE USER'S GUIDE

Daniel Mezick

The Open Agile Adoption Handbook

Open Agile Adoption™ is a trademark of Daniel Mezick

Revision Number: 1.0

Copyright © 2013 by Daniel Mezick

All rights reserved. No part of this book may be reproduced or transmitted in any form or by any means without written permission from the author.

ISBN (9780-0-9848753-2-0)

ACKNOWLEDGEMENTS

Time to thank some great people. There are many great people who have helped along the way, in developing Open Agile Adoption. The first is **Mike Loftus**, the very first client who was willing to take a shot with Open Space inside a large Agile adoption program. I'm grateful to you Mike, for granting me the authorization to make that first one happen.

The second person that needs a huge thank you is **Harrison Owen**, the author of many books on Open Space, and in particular the book *SPIRIT: Development and Transformation in Organizations*. I studied the book *SPIRIT* for the 1st time in early 2010 and that experience changed everything. Thank you Harrison Owen, and all the people in the Open Space community that have refined the Open Space format, and gifted the world with something great. Thanks to all of you, especially **Michael Herman** for his insightful writings on the power of invitation.

The next person that needs a huge shout of gratitude is **Mark Katz** of the American Society of Composers, Artists and Publishers, another of my clients. And a key one. Thanks Mark for being a great client, and for being an amazing leader of people, and for going all the way with Open Agile Adoption in service to your organization.

Thanks to everyone at www.AgileBoston.org who in any way, at any time, was party to the many public Open Space events we convened from 2008 to 2012 in Boston. Special thanks to **Pablo Pernot** and **Oana Juncu** for inviting me to keynote the 2013 Scrum Gathering in Paris, the invitation that created the motivation to formally explain and formalize the Open Agile Adoption technique.

Lastly I thank **Roberta Louise Mezick**, my wife and true friend, for totally getting who and what I am, and for supporting me all the way in everything I do.

From North Guilford, Connecticut, on September 6, 2013

Daniel Mezick

TABLE OF CONTENTS

INTRODUCTION	1
1. OPEN AGILE ADOPTION™: EXECUTIVE SUMMARY	7
2. OPEN AGILE ADOPTION IN THEORY	
Topics:	
Engagement and Game Mechanics	11
Liminality and the Stress of Transitions	14
Progress and Passage Rites	15
Communitas	19
The Master of Ceremonies	21
3. OPEN AGILE ADOPTION IN PRACTICE	
Topics:	
Preparing for Open Agile Adoption	25
Open Agile Adoption Steps	28
Beginning in Open Space	36
The Middle Phase: Experimentation and Storytelling	39
Ending in Open Space	45
APPENDIX A: SELECTED BIBLIOGRAPHY	51
APPENDIX B: ABOUT THE AUTHOR	53

INTRODUCTION

The Purpose of This Handbook

Welcome to the Open Agile Adoption Handbook. The purpose of this handbook is to serve as a handy reference and pocket guide for those who are adopting Agile, or otherwise using the Open Agile Adoption technique to bring strength and vitality to their Agile adoption effort.

Who This Book Is For

This book is for anyone who is interested in creating more rapid and lasting Agile adoptions. The list of people who can best use this book includes company executives, directors, managers, team members, and the consultants and coaches who serve them.

Preparing To Use This Book

This book assumes the following about you:

- You have a basic understanding of Agile methods, and how they can help your organization

- You have a basic understanding of the Open Space meeting format

- You are ready, willing and able to try the Open Agile Adoption technique to improve the results you are getting

INTRODUCTION

About the SPIRIT Book

It is important for all readers to understand that the Open Agile Adoption technique is inspired by the work of Harrison Owen and specifically his book *SPIRIT: Development and Transformation in Organizations*. That book is a great and mighty work. It is full of keen insights and actionable ideas. The SPIRIT book is of strong interest to anyone who is serious about culture architecture and culture design.

The SPIRIT book is available as a free download, in PDF format. I recommend that you download this book, print it out, and get it into a ring binder so you can mark it up as you read it.

You can find it here: http://www.openspaceworld.com/Spirit.pdf

The back of the book contains a Bibliography of additional books on topics related to Open Agile Adoption; if you are interested in some of the related topics it is a good idea to examine the titles listed there.

If you are seeking training in Open Agile Adoption or additional help in the form of consulting, you can also find that information in the back of the book. You can also learn more at www.OpenAgileAdoption.com.

Why Open Agile Adoption?

Open Agile Adoption is a technique based on invitation, not mandates. A hypothesis of Open Agile Adoption is that mandates reduce engagement, and that invitation and opt-in participation increase it. Another hypothesis of Open Agile Adoption is that engagement is essential for a rapid and lasting Agile adoption, and that Open Space tends to invite engagement and thereby increase it.

Typically, Agile practices are implemented as a mandate. Prescribing practices makes no allowance for what people want, what people think, and what people feel. The prescription reduces engagement and causes the intelligent and creative people who do the work to "check out" and disengage.

INTRODUCTION

Usually, the following pattern is used to implement Agile methods, usually after a small pilot test of Agile with a small team:

- Authority says we are all "going Agile"

- Authority says we will be using a specific practice, like Scrum, or Kanban, or some other Agile practice, method, or framework. The message is that this is not negotiable.

- Authority selects a coach on the basis of his or her expertise with the prescribed practices. Typically, Scrum skills. The coach is imposed on the people, just like the prescribed Agile practices.

  o The people who do the work are triggered to disengage by the experience of a low sense of control and a low sense of inclusion and belonging. They learn that the new game is vague, and participating is definitely not opt-in. *The Agile adoption is not an enjoyable game* because the game is not well defined, and there is no opportunity to opt-out.

Participation in the typical Agile adoption is *not* an invitation but rather a *mandate* and a *prescription*. This is a recipe for a *failed* Agile adoption. Recall that a hypothesis of Open Agile Adoption is that mandates reduce engagement, and that invitation and opt-in participation increase it. Also recall that another hypothesis of the technique is that *engagement is essential* for a rapid and lasting Agile adoption.

The people who create software programs typically have these characteristics, especially compared to the general population:

- High level of intelligence

- A tendency to be introverted

- A self image that includes these stories:

  o "I get paid to solve problems"

  o "I am smart and creative"

  o "I get paid for my technology expertise"

Mandated Agile adoptions tend to be repulsive to the intelligent, problem solving people that do the work. One reason might be that these folks literally *love* to solve problems, including "process problems", like "how to implement Agile at our company." Now, since most of the folks are introverted, if we do not ask them what they think, something really terrible happens: they *do not tell us*.

Often, the very people who do the work, these problem solvers, have an opinion or an idea that can help. By not asking them for help and instead issuing a prescribed mandate, we miss an opportunity to receive help, and also create the potential for considerable resentment. This is a double-barreled negative outcome. We miss what might be the very best ideas, and we miss a huge opportunity to engage.

A core hypothesis of Open Agile Adoption is that *engagement* is essential, and that *invitation* can increase it.

Instead of issuing a mandate of specific Agile practices, Open Agile Adoption employs this pattern, based in invitation:

- Explain the business case for moving in the Agile direction. Explain the challenges the business is facing in terms of competition, pricing pressure, obsolete products etc.

- Make it clear the enterprise is heading into an Agile direction. Explain that the Agile direction is definite.

- Invite *everyone* involved into the process of writing the Agile story. Communicate that leadership *does not* have all the answers and is *looking for the very best ideas people have* to make the move to Agile genuine, authentic, rapid, and lasting.

- Make it plain that everything that is tried as an Agile practice is an experiment, and is optional, and is going to be inspected, and is not set in stone. For example, if the org is giving the Scrum framework a try, it is an experiment, and subject to later inspection. If an off-the-rack practice like Scrum cannot be tailored and customized to fit well, it will be discarded, and we will try something else that might work. We might even "roll our own" practices, using the Agile Manifesto as our guidance.

By doing it this way, the people doing the work can engage, and have a strong sense of control and of progress.

Open Agile Adoption Terminology

The following terms and words are employed in this book, so you might want to take a moment to examine these definitions:

Liminality: A stressful state of being created by transitions. Agile adoptions create liminality.

Passage Rite: A ritual for handling the stress of change inside a culture. Passage rites help handle the liminality created during changes in status.

Communitas: The spirit of community. Open Agile Adoption creates these feelings of belonging and inclusion.

Master of Ceremonies: An essential role in a rite of passage. The person occupying the Master of Ceremonies role during a passage rite functions as a kind of referee, a keeper of "the rules of the game".

Chapter of learning: In Open Agile Adoption, a unit of organizational learning with a clear beginning, middle, and end. Chapters of learning occur between occurrences of Open Space meetings.

Open Space: A meeting format with a specific structure and containing specific elements. Periodic Open Space meetings are an essential and core aspect of Open Agile Adoption.

Open Space Proceedings: Documentation of the events contained within an Open Space meeting. Proceedings contain a summary of the events in words, diagrams, and pictures.

Open Space Sponsor: A person in the organization with enough authorization to convene an Open Space meeting of at least one day in duration.

Open Space Facilitator: In the Open Space meeting format, a person authorized by the Sponsor to assist in the execution of the meeting.

Open Space facilitators help to create an atmosphere of openness and "hold the space" open throughout the Open Space meeting event.

Coach or "Agile Coach": A person hired by the organization to assist in the implementation of Agile methods and practices.

Beginning Open Space: In Open Agile Adoption, an Open Space meeting that begins or opens a Chapter of learning.

Ending Open Space: In Open Agile Adoption, an Open Space meeting that completes and terminates a Chapter of learning.

Leveling Up: In the gaming community, the term is used to describe a change in level or status in the game. "Leveling up" means progressing or graduating to a new level of competence.

With these terms and words introduced we can now examine Open Agile Adoption concepts and facilities.

CHAPTER ONE

OPEN AGILE ADOPTION: EXECUTIVE SUMMARY

Open Agile Adoption (OAA) is a repeatable technique for getting a rapid and lasting Agile adoption. It works with what you are currently doing, and can be added at any time. It incorporates the power of invitation, Open Space, passage rites, game mechanics, storytelling and more, so your Agile adoption can take root. A hypothesis of Open Agile Adoption is increases in engagement drives increases in productivity, after a brief delay. The purpose of Open Agile Adoption is to increase levels of engagement on the part of everyone involved.

The core concept of OAA is the passage rite or "passage rite". A passage rite is a cultural event (and a kind of social game) that helps people make sense of complex transitions. Agile adoptions are complex transitions.

These are the key events in the passage rite:

- A Beginning: An Open Space meeting

- The Middle: With experimentation, play, and storytelling

- The End: An Open Space meeting

INTRODUCTION

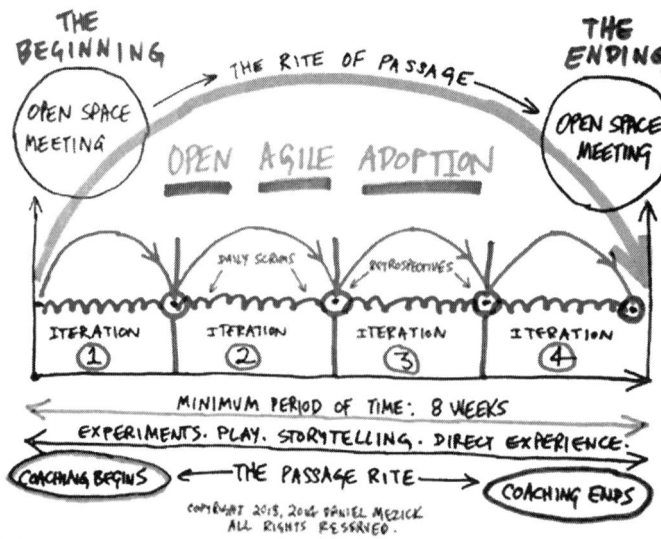

Figure 1: Open AGILE ADOPTION

OAA implements a structured rite of passage of several months duration, which begins and ends with an optionally attended Open Space meeting. In between, in the middle, all work is framed as experimentation. It is framed as playful experimentation that will be inspected by everyone involved, in several months, at the ending Open Space event. In other words, in the middle phase, the teams are encouraged to "play" with specific Agile practices, and to "act as if" these Agile practices can actually work. During this phase they are reminded that another Open Space meeting is planned and that everyone is invited to attend.

The beginning and ending Open Space events are essential, and form the containing structure. This structure has clear boundaries and helps to handle the anxiety generated by cultural change.

After the beginning Open Space, and inside the middle phase of the passage rite, additional components of Open Agile Adoption are used. An Agile coach functions as the master of ceremonies throughout. Executive storytelling is employed frequently, to help define what is happening and to remind everyone about the goal of continuous improvement. Game mechanics are used to help convey clear goals, rules, feedback mechanisms, and reiterate that participation in the Agile adoption game is optional.

This last point is essential: Open Agile Adoption is a technique based on invitation, not mandates. A hypothesis of Open Agile Adoption is that mandates reduce engagement, and that invitation and opt-in participation increase it. Another hypothesis of Open Agile Adoption is that engagement is essential, and that Open Space helps to increase it.

The end of the passage rite is punctuated with an event: the closing Open Space meeting. This closing meeting is the formal end-point in a "chapter of learning" in the life of the organization. It is also the opening of the next chapter.

In Open Agile Adoption, the coach assisting you plays an important role by providing guidance and teaching. The closing Open Space meeting is the place where the role of the Agile coach changes. At the closing the role of the coach must change. The coach may exit the organization, or move away from coaching teams and towards coaching executives. A new coach may replace the current coach. In any event, the status and authority of the coach must decrease. This reduction in coach status (and coach authority) is practical and symbolic.

In practical terms, the organization is now thinking much more independently, and is much more responsible for its own learning. In symbolic terms, this change in coach status is essential, and emphasized throughout the passage rite process, to underscore the fact that the organization is in fact making progress integrating agile ideas into the cultural fabric of the organization.

The Events in January and July

The last aspect of Open Agile Adoption is the twice-yearly Open Space meeting event. Held in January and July, these events are important and essential. They are anticipated by the organization as a whole, and serve as a place of cultural initiation for new hires.

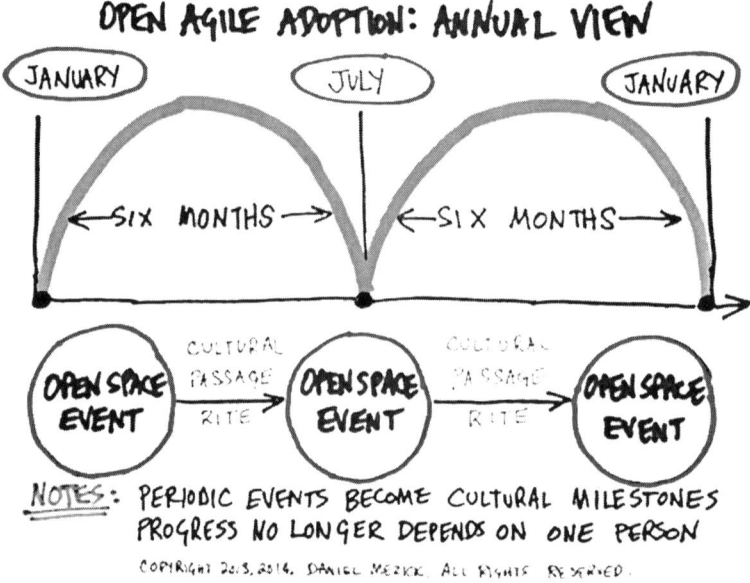

Figure 2: Open Agile Adoption Annual View

By instituting these recurring cultural events on the organization's calendar, the risk of dependency on any one leader is greatly reduced and might even be eliminated. A typical failure pattern in the adoption of Agile occurs when a highly authorized sponsor and progressive leader exits the company. The 'safe space' necessary to do Agile well departs with him or her. By instituting these recurring, twice-per-year Open Space events, the process of Agile transformation can and will continue, regardless of who is currently occupying the formally authorized leadership roles.

CHAPTER TWO

OPEN AGILE ADOPTION IN THEORY

Introduction

OAA is built on some core ideas from the psychology of games and cultural anthropology. These are described in some detail below. It is important to understand the theory of OAA before implementing it, so be sure to examine this chapter carefully.

Good Games: Goals, Rules, Feedback, and Opt-In Participation

Happiness at work is a game. If the core requirements for happiness at work are not present, you disengage and check out. If the core requirements are there, you automatically experience fun, satisfaction and potentially, a deeply engaged sense of well-being. Open Agile adoption delivers happiness through the intentional design and implementation of good-game mechanics.

Work is BROKEN when it is not fun to play. You are delivering happiness at work by injecting good-game mechanics into the structure of work and meetings.

- The core requirements for happiness at work are:
- A sense of control
- A sense of progress
- A sense of belonging and membership
- A sense of wider purpose and meaning

When viewed in this way, it is possible to more fully game your interactions, your meetings and work itself, so that participating is optimized towards a satisfying, fun and naturally productive experience.

Open Agile Adoption is employs game mechanics to make your Agile adoption enjoyable and fun.

Games

Games have four basic properties. When the values for each of the properties are "well-formed", the game is enjoyable, fun and satisfying. When the four properties are not "well-formed", the game is not fun and you either opt-out or, if this is not possible, you disengage ("check out") almost automatically.

The 4 basic properties of a good game are:

- A clear goal
- A clear set of rules that are uniformly applied
- A clear way to get feedback, to track progress
- Opt-in participation

Well-executed Agile patterns and practices are usually (but not always) well-formed games. Well-formed games associate with satisfaction, happiness and even joyfulness; poorly defined games associate with disengagement, low levels of learning, and a distinct lack of enjoyment.

Open Agile adoption makes culture change easier by making it a good game. The key gaming component is the invitation, which is used instead of a mandate. Participants are invited to experiment with Agile practices, instead of being forced to use them without being part of the decision making process.

Culture is a game, and Agile culture is no exception. Agile adoptions are games. To make Agile adoptions fun, we must tune up four properties: the goals, the rules, the feedback loops, and the ability to opt in or out of playing the game. In Open Agile Adoption, a focus on game mechanics is essential.

Invitation: Opt-In Participation... Instead of a Mandate

Mandates reduce engagement. They have the potential to ruin your Agile adoption. The mandate of Agile practices reduces the potential for genuine engagement.

Invitation increases engagement by offering options and choice. A sense of control and a sense of belonging are sources of basic human happiness. Opting in or out of an invitation increases the sense of control. Accepting an invitation increases the sense of belonging and inclusion.

Mandating Agile practices seldom works because there is no opt-in feature to the game. This makes it less than fun to play. The game is not "well-formed." This may seem counterintuitive. Mandates reduce engagement, the very fuel of rapid and lasting Agile adoptions. Invitation is a far better approach, and aligns with the Agile Manifesto's core principles.

Consider these quotes from Martin Fowler, a signatory of the Agile Manifesto:

> A team may choose a totally waterfall, un-agile process. In that case, clearly the process is no more agile than apples taste of strawberries. But agile methods aren't the best for all situations, and personally I'd rather have a team work in a non-agile manner they chose themselves than have my favorite agile practices imposed upon them.
>
> -Martin Fowler, Agile Manifesto signatory, the "Agile Imposition" blog post, 2006

Here are more quotes, from that same essay:

> "Imposing an agile process from the outside strips the team of the self-determination which is at the heart of agile thinking."
>
> "... imposing agile methods introduces a conflict with the values and principles that underlie agile methods."
>
> "So I hope I've made clear that imposing agile methods is a very red flag."

Open Agile Adoption is a good game, in part because of the opt-in feature, which we know is an essential of any good game. Invitation has the potential to engage the independent thinkers in your organization, the very people who can help create success with Agile.

CHAPTER TWO

Liminality and Learning

The *liminal* state is a transitional state of being. The root Latin word- limens- means "threshold". The liminal state is a no-mans land of transition, confusion, stress and vagueness. It is lacking in definition. No longer where you were, and not yet where you will end up, liminality literally has the potential to drive you crazy.

Liminality is a stressful state of being that occurs in transitions. Agile adoptions are, by definition, liminal in nature. Agile adoptions generate considerable worry and anxiety. Open Agile Adoption uses a well-understood cultural device called the "passage rite" to manage liminality and reduce stress.

The Relationships between Agile, Liminality and Learning

Adopting Agile always means lots and lots of new learning. Learning is stressful, because it generates liminality. All genuine learning in adults creates instability- *liminality*- until that learning is integrated.

On Mental Models

We know the world through our models. Mature adults hold a model of reality. Genuine new learning challenges the validity of that model. This invalidation of your previous assumptions produces the very unstable, liminal state, until you integrate that new learning.

The introduction of Agile into an organization definitely creates liminality. The introduction of Agile is usually quite triggering for most participants. This "triggered" behavior is based on fear, and is a natural reaction to entering the unstable state of liminality.

Before Agile, everything was well understood. Then: ...new roles, new ways of interacting, and a new mindset are all required of you. The learning is constant, and stressful. Agile can be very triggering.

Uncomfortable in the transition, the natural and safe thing to do is turn around and go back to where you came from. And people in organizations routinely do exactly this. We backslide on Agile and return to where we came from. This "going back" reduces the worry, the fear and the anxiety, the core emotions evoked by the liminal state of being.

Rites of Passage

Passage rites have been used for thousands of years to manage stressful transitions in human systems. Open Agile Adoption implements a passage rite that begins and ends with an Open Space meeting event. This brings structure to the chaos associated with the integration of new learning.

Various tribal societies, throughout the world, across different periods of time, and coming from different places, have all come to the exact same conclusion: liminality must be carefully handled, and the best way to handle it is to institute a passage rite.

The purpose of a passage rite is to ease the transition from one state of being... to another. Tribal societies have been doing this routinely, for thousands of years.

In the modern day, we routinely introduce Agile into organizations, while blissfully ignoring the essential human dynamics of liminality.

This is probably a very serious error.

CHAPTER TWO

Stability in the Liminal State

A hypothesis of Open Agile Adoption is that introducing Agile into typical organizations creates liminality at the group level. If this liminality is handled with a passage rite, there is potential for a rapid and lasting Agile adoption.

The core idea behind Open Agile Adoption is that recognizing and addressing liminality reduces the worry, anxiety and fear associated with Agile adoption. It creates at least the potential for a rapid and lasting Agile adoption. The primary way this is accomplished is by leveraging the ancient practice of the passage rite. A passage rite creates a structured experience for participants....with a beginning, a middle and an end.

Open Agile Adoption is a repeatable technique for getting a rapid and lasting Agile adoption. It works with what you are currently doing, and can be added at any time. It incorporates passage rites, game mechanics, Open Space, storytelling and more, so your Agile adoption can take root.

The Passage Rite

Transitions are tough, and serve as a kind of bridge from here to there. Adopting Agile is a big transition that always means lots and lots of new learning. And learning is stressful, because it generates liminality.

All genuine learning in adults creates instability- *liminality*- until that learning is integrated. The primary way to manage liminality in a social system is to institute a passage rite.

A rite of passage provides a structure. This ritual has a structure that provides a beginning, middle and an end to a transitional experience.

Experience Design

Designing a passage rite is an exercise in experience design. Passage rites contain and thereby reduce the highly destabilizing feelings of liminality. This is important, because liminality causes stress that can lead to all sorts of problems, including deep anxiety, fear, panic, depression and even various forms of neuroses.

When you study passage rites, you learn that they usually include at least one very scary experience. For example: a member of a tribe in Africa going through a passage rite from boyhood to manhood might have to kill a dangerous animal, like a lion or a hyena. You might be wondering if this passage-rite notion is such a good idea. Do we really want to put people though super-scary experiences?

Here is something to think about: culturally speaking, what comes first: the highly stressful transition, or the passage rite?

Passage Rites and Liminality

The highly stressful transition comes first. Passage rites are a cultural response. Passage rites serve to contain the scary experience of transition. They are established by a culture in response to the need for management of highly stressful liminality. The transition comes first; the creation of a passage rite comes later, as a cultural mechanism for managing the transition from here to there.

In other words, a passage rite does not produce liminality. Instead a passage rite manages the liminality that shows during key transitions in the life of the group and its members.

The stressful and necessary transition- for example, the transition from childhood to adulthood- is present BEFORE a passage rite was instituted.

The primary task of of a structured passage rite is to ease the stressful liminality created by a transition.

The primary task of an Agile adoption is to produce a cultural transformation. This is a huge transition that in theory never ever ends, because it is focused on continuous learning and improvement.

We currently do not manage this very *huge* transition as well as we might. Passage rites can help.

And that is what Open Agile Adoption is all about.

Passage Rites as Culture Games

Passage rites are cultural games. They are designed with a clear goal, clear rules, rich feedback, and opt-in participation. It is important to note that the Open Agile Adoption technique is instituting passage rite, and that this passage rite is in fact a game!

Key Points:

- Big transitions in the life of a group produce liminality;

- Liminality is stressful. It can make you anxious and fearful;

- Passage rites do not produce liminality, instead passage rites are cultural devices that help handle the liminal state of being, so that the participants can *get through*... to go where they need to go.

- Agile adoptions are transitions and produce considerable anxiety, worry and the liminal state;

- A formal passage rite- a certain kind of cultural ritual- can help;

- Open Agile Adoption works because it acknowledges these dynamics, and institutes a rite of passage that helps all the participants in an Agile adoption get from where they are... to where they need to go;

- Passage rites are designed games that emerge from necessity in a culture, to help it thrive.

Play and Experimentation

Let's just tell it like it is: Agile is a learning framework that is based on frequent experimentation. All experimentation is play. Therefore, Agile is learning is playful. Open Agile Adoption supports and strongly encourages experimentation and genuine playfulness. OAA frames Agile experience as a series of *experiments*. What is really going on is play. And play is fun.

Communitas

Agile adoptions thrive on strong feelings of communitas. Communitas is "the spirit of community". When the spirit of community is "up", the space is open, and the feeling of communitas is strong. When the spirit of community is "down", the space is closed, and the communitas is weak.

Example: If you love going to work, the overall spirit at work is probably "up". If you cannot wait till Friday, the overall spirit in that workplace is probably "down".

With respect to Agile adoptions, *communitas* is essential. It comes from clearly understood and uniformly applied rules. It comes from a sense that everyone is engaged. It comes from a sense that we are all going through this together.

During Agile adoptions, everyone is being triggered. What is my role? What are the rules? When does this end? What does this mean for my status in the group? Executive leaders are triggered. Managers are triggered. Team members are triggered. A new game with new rules is stressful. In a no-man's land of new rules, new roles and unfamiliar ways of working, is it any wonder Agile adoptions routinely fail?

Passage rites can help generate *communitas*- the very spirit of community. Cultural anthropology says that people going through a passage rite do in fact have the same status during the passage. Participants have widely varied status, going in.

Then the communitas kicks in: all are coming from a known place, and going to an unknown place. All of them make the difficult and even dangerous passage, together. And after it is over, all have changed from what they were, to what they now are. Passage rites can help ease the liminality of transition.

Passage rites are intentionally designed cultural experiences. Repeat: Passage rites are intentionally designed cultural experiences. They are cultural-experience designs. Passage rites are designed to create feelings of community.

Agile adoptions generate a steady stream of stressful liminality, because the learning in Agile is constant. "Continuous improvement" is the goal. That generates a ton of stress on your culture. Learning is change, and change is stressful because it produces liminality. The passage rite is a cultural device for handling liminality.

Passage rites bring communitas, and communitas brings at least some (and maybe more than a little comfort.) All the participants going through the passage rite experience a beginning, a middle, and an end. They experience it together, regardless of level of authorization. Everyone is learning.

This structuring of the unstructured is very comforting, and reduces worries– and stress. Passage rites are extremely useful devices for helping you obtain a rapid and lasting Agile adoption.

Open Agile Adoption is a repeatable technique for getting a rapid and lasting Agile adoption. It works with what you are currently doing, and can be added at any time. It incorporates the power of invitation, Open Space, passage rites, game mechanics, storytelling and more, so your Agile adoption can take root.

Open Space: Passion and Responsibility

The Open Space meeting format is designed to generate very high levels of engagement. It does so by getting all the people with a sense of passion and responsibility in one place, at one time, to address matters of importance to all participants. Open Agile Adoption uses Open Space to generate invitation, and engagement.

The Master of Ceremonies

Every legitimate rite of passage is a designed cultural experience and Open Agile Adoption is no exception. Part of the design is the 'Master of Ceremonies' role.

The Master of Ceremonies is an essential role in the passage rite event. The Master of Ceremonies helps to maintain the structure and makes sure that the passage rite is executed well. The Master of Ceremonies is a kind of referee that works in service to everyone experiencing the liminal state of transition. In Open Agile Adoption, the person in the Coach role functions as the Master of Ceremonies during the passage rite.

It is important to note here that the Sponsor cannot act as the Master of Ceremonies. This is because the Sponsor is actually a participant with everyone else, in the passage rite.

Storytelling

> "...the name of the game is Collective Storytelling. This process may begin with the leader's tale." (Harrison Owen, The SPIRIT Book, p. 112)

In Open Agile Adoption, deliberate storytelling is essential. Story telling is well understood to be essential to the generation of culture. In OAA, leaders engage in deliberate acts of narrative creation with a specific focus on telling stories using past tense, present tense and future tense.

Semiotics & Signaling

We navigate the world via signs and signals. In organizations, how leaders behave the primary signal. Leaders provide signals about where we are, and where we are going. We look for these signs and signals, and use them to navigate. Inside an Open Agile Adoption, leaders integrate the idea of *signaling* into everything they do. People tell stories about leader behavior. In Open Agile Adoption, leaders are "tuned in." to storytelling.

Stories are signals and signage in a culture.

The Sense of Progress: The Coach Role Changes over Time

In OAA, a segment of learning bounded by two Open Space events is called a Chapter. Each Chapter represents a passage, and progress. In Open Agile Adoption, the role of the Coach changes formally at the end of each Chapter. This creates a sense of graduating and "leveling up".

Announcing the fact that the Coach role is going to change as of the next Open Space meeting is an essential aspect of OAA. This announcement signals that the teams and everyone else involved needs to get busy assuming more and more responsibility for taking the Agile adoption forward.

It is essential that the role of the coach diminish with each Chapter that starts and ends in Open Space. This reduction in the authority of the Coach has a symbolic and practical aspect. In practical terms, the teams must know that the coach cannot be depended upon to answer all questions forever, and that they must mature to the point where they need little (if any) coaching to continuously improve. In symbolic terms, the reduction of the authority of the Coach means that the teams are assuming at least some (if not all) of the authority the Coach originally started with.

With each Open Space event, the authority of the Coach is decreasing formally. This is important for delivering a periodic and strong sense of progress across the entire organization. Without this change is the status of the Coach, there is no progress and in fact no passage from here to there.

The entire job of the coach is to get the organization to a place where they are taking total responsibility for their own learning. This does not happen all at once.

Recurring Cultural Ritual

Open Agile Adoption implements a series of passage rites designed to enable a rapid and lasting Agile adoption. Each passage ritual begins and ends with an Open Space meeting. These rituals enable the group to reduce the stress associated with the transition to Agile.

What happens after that? In Open Agile Adoption, this pattern of the periodic passage rite literally becomes part of the culture. Genuine Agile creates at least the potential continuous learning. With continuous learning comes continuous liminality. A key feature of Open Agile Adoption is the institution of periodic and recurring Open Space meetings, typically in January and July each year. These meetings are cultural ceremonies- *rituals*. These meetings serve as milestones and important cultural checkpoints. The fixed scheduling of these events form a container for the learning and the liminality that comes with it. These cultural events support the continuous learning that an Agile culture creates. These cultural events in January and June also serve to initiate new hires into the organization's culture of learning.

CHAPTER THREE

OPEN AGILE ADOPTION IN PRACTICE

Preparing for Open Agile Adoption

Preparing for Open Agile Adoption is fairly straightforward. This section explains how.

As stated in the introduction of this book, I recommend that you obtain the book SPIRIT by Harrison Owen and read it very carefully. The Open Agile Adoption technique is an application of many of the ideas found in that book. The SPIRIT book describes a kind of cultural operating system; Open Agile Adoption is a kind of application that runs on it.

Assumptions: Authorization and Commitment of Sponsor

For OAA to work well, a committed and duly authorized sponsor is required. The person in the Sponsor role is pivotal: if they execute well, things go well. If they execute poorly, things go badly.

The Sponsor must be duly authorized. Without a duly authorized sponsor, there is no opportunity to effectively use OAA, because OAA is a process that requires and depends on explicit authorization.

The Sponsor must be committed to the OAA process. This means the Sponsor is willing to:

- Read about OAA in preparation

- Accept the guidance of a coach

- Follow the rules of the OAA game (as described in this book)

- Convey some specific authority for decision making to the teams

CHAPTER THREE

Teaching Open Agile Adoption

OAA is a learn-by-doing approach that leverages *invitation* as the primary device for creating engagement. Leaders, stakeholders and teams need some orientation beyond the usual Agile training and orientation that precedes adoption of Agile methods.

Teaching the Software People

The people that work inside the software teams need teaching on the following:

- The basics of the Agile Manifesto (4 values & 12 principles)

- The basics on the Agile practices (Scrum, Kanban etc)

Teaching the Executive Leaders

Leaders need teaching on:

- The Agile Manifesto (4 values and 12 principles)

- Open Space fundamentals

- What to expect from Open Agile Adoption

- The process of Open Agile Adoption

- How to handle surprising data and information

- How to leverage the power of storytelling

Storytelling & Signaling in Open Agile Adoption

It is very important for leaders to understand the concepts and facilities of OAA before getting started. OAA is a game, a game of transition from here to there. OAA implements a passage rite structure that is designed to smooth the process of moving from the existing culture to a more Agile culture. Leaders need to understand how to use the power of the passage rite and storytelling to address various kinds of situations that can and will come up during the process.

For more information on specific training for Agile teams and company leaders, please visit www.OpenAgileAdoption.com.

The Beginning Open Agile Adoption Step-by-Step

It is essential to frame all the Agile activity as experimental. This gets people "in". If this is not done, then the way the work is done is perceived as a pre-ordained and non-negotiable mandate. If the work is framed as an experiment to be inspected, then the people who do the work will feel a sense of progress through a process of inspection and adjustment.

A key practice in Agile work is the periodic and frequent inspection of recent experience. It is essential to make it plain that these inspections include the opportunity to discuss what is NOT working and eliminate it from the Agile practices being used. This makes it easy for people to "suspend disbelief" as they participate in the adoption-of-Agile process. The idea of periodically creating a space or venue where every idea and insight gets a hearing is a powerful one. When the people doing the work start to experience this, the experience includes a felt sense of control, the feeling of progress and a sense of belonging and communitas.

Regardless of whether you are just starting or well along in terms of executing on work in an Agile way, it is key and essential that everything be framed as an experiment. The general story you want people telling is a story about "commitment to experimentation". In service to that idea, try to use language like:

"…Each iteration is an experiment"

"…let's act as if" this might work

"…let's pretend" that this experiment (in an iteration for example) might work

"…let's suspend our disbelief long enough to try this out…"

The following is a high-level description of the sequence of steps in the Open Agile Adoption process. Planning Open Agile Adoption is an exercise in planning and executing on an *experience design*.

Here are the steps:

- Plan and Execute the Beginning Open Space Meeting
    - Step 1: Language and Rhetoric
    - Step 2: Schedule a Date and Location
    - Step 3: Craft the Open Space Meeting Theme
    - Step 4: Craft the Open Space Meeting Invitation
    - Step 5: Issuing the Invite and Socialize the Event.
    - Step 6: Execute on Planning; Name the Facilitator.
    - Step 7: Inspect Results From Initial Invitation
    - Step 8: Execute The Meeting
    - Step 9: Creation of Proceedings
- Plan and Execute on Agile Experimentation Inside Iterations
    - Step 10: Inspect And Act Upon Proceedings
    - Step 11: Teams Engage in Agile Experiments
    - Step 12: Leaders Engage in Storytelling
- Plan and Execute on the Ending Open Space Meeting
    - Step 13: Formally change the role of the Coach
- Inspect and Adapt
    - Step 14: Inspect Results; Repeat If Necessary

- Step 15: Institute Recurring Open Space in June and July

The following provides details on each step:

Step One: Language and Rhetoric

As discussed above, it is important to frame the Agile adoption experience as an experiment. The mandate is to get Agile going; the optional piece and the part that you invite everyone into is the act of trying various practices, dropping what is not working and carrying the successes forward. The key is for everyone to know that they have choices, and that they are being invited to "figure this out" and in effect, write the story of the Agile adoption.

Step Two: Schedule a Date and Location

Pick a day about 6 weeks out. Try to avoid arranging a date so PersonX or PersonY can attend. It is more important to get MOST of the people there. Delaying for individuals is not a good strategy. Set a firm date and move to the next step.

Step Three: Craft the Open Space Meeting Theme

Craft the theme. The theme defines the experience for participants. The theme frames the story of the event. The theme helps participants "know what it means." The theme is essential for sense making at the level of individual and group. The theme is always framed as a question such as "How Can We Help Each Other?" or "Why Agile Now?". The theme must be wide enough to handle diverse topics and narrow enough to clearly frame the experience for participants. The theme is an important structural element of the overall experience design.

Step Four: Craft the Open Space Meeting Invitation

The invitation further refines and explains and develops the theme. It has to:

- Reference the Theme

- Be short

- Be from a person duly authorized to convene the meeting, and

- Have some explanation of both the problems the group is facing as well as some good links that explain open space.

See the Appendices for a list of useful links on Open Space.

Step Five: Issuing The Invite and Socialize the Event.

Issuing the invite; socialize the event. The invite needs to be sent about 5 weeks in advance of the meeting. The practical minimum is about 4 weeks. Less than that does not provide adequate time for socializing the event. People need time to hear the story, think, do some research, talk to others about it, and make a decision to attend or not. Since Open Space does not demand anything of you beyond what you are willing to do, it is very easy to attend and simply play it passively. However what usually ends up happening is, people with a plan to play passive often end up playing actively as small-session Conveners, they play as participants in small-session conversations, and as occupants of other Open Space roles. Open Space has a way of helping peace and understanding to "break out".

Step Six: Execute on Planning and Logistics; Name the Facilitator.

The meeting starts and ends in a large circle, with small sessions convened in small groups throughout the day. The role of the Facilitator is key and essential. A skilled Facilitator helps you do preparation, and execute, and do the post-event follow up. Things to plan for include start and stop time, food and beverages, supplies, space preparation, proceedings, and post-meeting analysis and planning. These topics are well covered in the book listed above. Get a copy and use it for guidance in planning. Pick a Facilitator who has done at least one non-public (organizational) Open Space event. Private events that are specific to an organization and culture are very different from public events. Make sure your Facilitator has experience in a private setting specific to one organization. Make sure you have a clear plan for the collection and generation of written proceedings.

Step Seven: Inspect Results from Initial Invitation

Send the invite again about one week out. People usually wait till the last minute before committing to attendance. This is normal and to be expected the 1st time you run an Open Space event inside your organization. For this reason, expect to send out the invite again. Edit it slightly to reflect the context of being one week out, and then send it again. Provide a way for people to RSVP and commit to attendance so you can get a good count.

Step Eight: Execute

This is the easy part. The book *Open Space: A User's Guide* can help you. Your Facilitator provides all the guidance you need beyond that. The Sponsor (who sent the Invite and helped craft the Theme) speaks first, and explains the context, and introduces the Facilitator. The Facilitator takes it from there, explaining the roles, the rules of the Open Space game, and the process of creating and executing an agenda.

As explained by the Facilitator, no one attending is actually required to do anything. People may choose to convene sessions, or attend one session, or attend many sessions, or simply "hang out" in the space, eating the food and drinking beverages while conversing with people. Open Space is about people exercising their agency and choices. As a leader, you are sure to find people expressing themselves in the 'open space' that is created by this meeting. People not currently perceived as leaders "show up" as the champion of new ideas and concepts that participants find useful. Sometimes they show up as antagonists, people who inject energy into debating the relative merit of the current idea being considered in a session. The slogan "be prepared to be surprised" is a truism in Open Space.

Step Nine: Creation of Proceedings

As mentioned in the Planning step, the proceedings are essential. Don't leave this step out. Tangible proceedings become the source of plans for going forward. They also become important cultural artifacts that document the wider story of your Agile adoption over time. These documents are interesting to new people who join your organization. The proceedings tell the story and support the wider effort to grow more learning in your organization.

Step Ten: Inspect Proceedings

Inspecting proceedings is the big moment in OAA. The Open Space meeting happened, it was great, and the sessions generated new information for leaders and the teams. Now the people who have the passion and responsibility are waiting for formally authorized leaders to follow through.

It is quite likely new leaders identified they. It is quite likely that some of the problems identified in the Open Space need immediate attention. The proceedings make the results from the Open Space meeting real and tangible. Now it is time for the formally authorized leadership to take action. Do not wait! Generate proceedings as fast as possible and address the issues raised, without delay. This is a critical step. If leadership does not follow through with immediately addressing impediments and other issues raised during the Open Space, we can expect people to disengage. If we quickly address issues raised during the Open Space, we can expect great things to happen.

Step Thirteen: Formally change the role of the Coach

In Open Agile Adoption, the ending Open Space meeting closes a chapter of Agile learning and completes the structure of a formal passage rite with a formal beginning, a rather messy middle phase, and a formal ending.

It is very important for the role of the Coach to progressively change as each Chapter of learning is completed. Each Chapter is punctuated by an Open Space meeting. Prior to this meeting, everyone involved needs to be told how the Coach role will change. The Coach is to have progressively less and less authority in the situation as the teams and stakeholders gain competence. If the Coach role does not change, the teams and stakeholders will quite naturally continue to depend on the Coach to provide leadership, answer questions, and act in an authoritative way. Open Agile Adoption loosely implements the

Situational Leadership model as developed by Ken Blanchard. Before a Chapter of learning starts, the team and stakeholders are told that the Coach's role is changing. This has two immediate effects:

1. The teams and stakeholders will get busy figuring Agile out

2. The teams and stakeholders will feel a genuine sense of progress, like a kind of graduation or "leveling up", after the Chapter of learning is completed

In practice, the Coach's change in status can take many forms. A coach may start with coaching team practices, and then switch to doing that just one day a week, with the rest of the time spent coaching facilitators, product owners and others. In the next Chapter, they may move to coaching only formally authorized leaders. Exactly how the Coach role changes is less important than announcing that a change is going to happen, and making sure it happens as of the next Open Space meeting.

Step Fourteen: Inspect Results; Repeat If Necessary

Each organization is unique. Each has unique culture. No two organizations are the same. For this reason, you need to inspect the results from each Chapter with OAA. Some organizations need two Chapters of at least three months each. Some need only one. It's OK to repeat the process in three-month intervals at first. The rule is that the Coach cannot facilitate any Open Space meetings after the first one, because the Coach becomes viewed as an authority figure. Facilitators in Open Space function as servants of the group and have little if any authority.

Step Fifteen: Institute Recurring Open Space in June and July

The final step in the Open Agile Adoption process is to institute and install recurring Open Space meetings in July and January. These meetings, about 6 months apart, serve as more than retrospectives. The recurring meetings serve as important cultural events on the organizations annual calendar.

Here are some of the purposes of the recurring meetings:

- To initiate new hires into the culture

- To create a known and recurring time and place where everyone gets a hearing

- To close out a Chapter in the story of the organizations culture change

- To open a new Chapter

- To discuss & then discard habits & practices that are no longer useful

- To discuss and then more widely adopt practices that are working well

- To put the culture in charge of evolving itself, instead of depending on one leader or group of leaders

- To demonstrate the holding of the core values of learning, in service to rapidly adapting to change

Open Agile Adoption Steps: Summary

As noted above, the very first Open Space event you run does not close out a previous Chapter of learning. Instead that first Open Space marks the place of the beginning.

Subsequent Open Space meetings serve a dual purpose: they ritually and ceremonially close the current Chapter of learning, and open a new Chapter.

The function of ritual and ceremony cannot be understated in this context. Open Space events are good places for a formal rotation of coaches and/or a change in the coaching role. The Open Space event is a wonderful place for the current coach to exit, and to "graduate" the team members and everyone else to a new level, to a new chapter and a new level of mastery and understanding. In this very real sense, the Open Agile Adoption process is a rite of passage for your teams and your organization.

After the event, it is important to note the tone, tempo, and learning that came from the meeting. New ideas (or old ideas whose time has now arrived) need to be supported.

Old ways of working need to be put aside. The lessons learned can (and in fact must be) integrated into future plans.

Open Space provides a signal event that creates *containment*-- and brings meaning to the often-turbulent experience of rapid team and organizational learning.

CHAPTER THREE

Notes on the Beginning Open Space Meeting

The beginning Open Space meeting opens a passage rite process led by the Coach. The leaders and the people on the teams are starting something new. The beginning Open Space meeting marks the opening of this process.

The Goals of the First Open Space Meeting

This meeting has several goals (not ranked or ordered):

- To mark the beginning of a Chapter of learning
- To give everyone an opportunity to be heard
- To serve as a signal event that is signaling openness
- To introduce the Open Space meeting format
- To demonstrate how additional Open Space meetings will feel
- To generate ideas for action as soon as the meeting is over
    - To generate proceedings available to all
- To identify emergent leadership:
    - In Open Space, people you might not normally associate with leadership often demonstrate leadership in many ways. Open Space helps identify people who can help your Agile adoption succeed.

- To explain that this opens a Chapter of learning, and that another Open Space meeting already scheduled at least 90 days in the future closes the Chapter

- To explain that the Coach is going to behave in a specific way after this meeting, and that after the next Open Space meeting, the status and behavior of the coach will change.

Role of the Coach

The coach may optionally play the role of Open Space Facilitator during the 1st Open Space. This helps to establish the Coach as the Master of Ceremonies. The Coach explains Open Space, facilitates the event and make sure everyone knows at the closing of this meeting that another meeting, just like this one, is planned in 8 to 12 weeks. The Coach also explains at the closing of this meeting that the work that follows (using Agile practices) is experimental in nature and that the teams are going to say whatever they want to say about these practices at the ending Open Space meeting that is planned in 8 to 12 weeks.

The Meeting Theme and Invitation

The Open Space theme is very important and must be crafted by the organization's leaders... and in fact *all of those with a real stake in the success of the Agile adoption.* It is a good idea to issue an invite to everyone to attend a pre-meeting to discuss the importance of the Open Space meeting theme, and to participate in defining it. This helps to create some buzz and get everyone engaged. It is better for the people who are doing the work to craft the theme, consistent with the goals and objectives for the Agile adoption.

The Open Space theme is always framed as a question, because questions tend to "open the space", while directives and so-called statements of fact tend to "close the space".

Themes I have seen organizations select include the following:

"How can we help each other?"
"What does it mean for us to be Agile?"
"Agile at [Company Name]: In Service to What?"

Any decent question can work; in every case make sure the crafting of it is a team sport and not decided by one person. The more people involved the better where the theme is concerned.

Once the theme is selected the next step is the development of the invitation.

The Meeting Invite

The meeting invitation for Open Space provides some development of the theme for interested parties who may choose to attend. In general, the less said the better. The invite is informed by the theme, and provides some clues about what is important. Much has been written on how to craft an Open Space invitation, so I refer you to the books and web pages listed in the Appendices for more information on crafting the Open Space theme and related invitation.

Clarity on Next Meeting

A central principle of the OAA approach is that the Coach role changes in a public and formal way as part of each Open Space. Going in, everyone knows the person in Coach role is going to have a reduction of conferred authority inside the organization. The idea here is to signal (in both symbolic and practical terms) that the organization is maturing and changing for the better, and therefore can be less and less dependent on the Coach for guidance, answers and so on.

This must be well communicated at all times. The change in Coach status is a rule change, a rule change in the game of the Agile adoption. With each Open Space, the Coach moves further and further away from the original role (and higher level of authorization) they previously occupied.

It's important to note that the status of the Coach changes.

Notes on the Middle Phase: Experimentation & Storytelling

The middle phase between the Open Space is where teams do Agile experiments and play, and leaders tell stories.

The Middle Phase, for Teams

The first Open Space sets the stage for play. The middle phase between the two Open Space meeting are where the teams experiment and play with Agile. The word "play" is a loaded term, and is often posed as an opposite of "work".

Briefly: play is what people do when they are learning. The sanitized term is 'experimentation." It is essential that everyone (doing any Agile practices whatsoever in the middle phase) understand that they are playing. It is the proper role of leadership to communicate this, through storytelling. They key here is to communicate that if a practice is not working well, it will be discarded. The teams need to have the sense of control that comes from this knowledge. The alternative is to communicate that the practices are mandated, with the predictable disengagement that comes from feelings of loss of control.

The entire idea behind OAA is to reduce the worry that comes from new processes and roles in the workplace. The simplest way to reduce these worries is to frame everything as an experiment to be inspected. This is not only aligned with common sense but also with Agile principles as described in the Agile Manifesto itself.

A hypothesis of OAA is that introducing Agile changes into your organization can be very triggering for participants. With this in mind, during the middle phase of an OAA Chapter of learning, leaders tell stories that confirm and validate and continue the spirit of openness generated by the previous Open Space event.

The Middle Phase, for Leaders

Leaders are signaling devices in organizations. The signal they send can open and can also close space. The signals that leaders send are used by observers to learn what is valued and also to learn how to navigate the social terrain. Leaders can signal with verbal and non-verbal communications, and in writing.

Psychological safety is the safety to take interpersonal risks. Safe space is space that is open to speak honestly about what you think and feel. Space that is safe allows the best idea to appear and get identified and processed.

Leaders set the tone and tempo regarding psychological safety. After an Open Space meeting, the Proceedings are delivered to all participants and they must be processed by formally authorized leadership. The entire purpose of producing the Proceedings (and immediately processing them) is to *extend* the safe space created during the Open Space meeting event. A primary way leaders can expend psychological safety is through direct action (which generates stories) and storytelling (which generates signals and signs)

Leadership Storytelling in Open Agile Adoption

Everyone loves a good story and stories are told and retold in organizations. Stories are powerful sociocultural tools. In OAA, storytelling is essential. Leaders tell stories in the past, present and future tenses.

Past, Present & Future Tense Stories

The basic idea with storytelling is to build the future story on the present story, and to build the present story upon stories about the past. It is essential to do this in Open Agile Adoption. We are telling a new story about a new cultural game. The name of the new game is Openness, and that means trouble for the old story and the old game.

Stories about the Past

No matter how bad the past was, there is always something good in it. The first step in storytelling is to validate the past, and tell a good story about it. For example, if the culture is closed, and psychological safety is low, if you look you can find a time when there was more openness. Perhaps the origin story of the enterprise includes a period when it was do or die, and everyone did everything. Look for that story, and use it as a foundation to build the new story. It is essential to validate the past. Avoid any invalidation the past is essential. Always tie the story about the present to the past, and build on it. Find something good from the past, refer to it, and build the present-tense story upon it.

Present-tense stories are celebrations of current successes. As teams gain competency, it is important to encourage them. When formally authorized leaders celebrate recent successes, the teams can and will do better. More importantly, If you are a formally authorized leader, your stories are having an effect upon everyone in the space. Your stories are signaling what is valued. This is an important signal that is attractive to some receivers and repulsive to others. If for example you tell a story about how a team got some good results by experimenting, you are sending the signal that experimenting inside teams is valued. One side effect of this is that people who do not value experimentation become less comfortable. Keep in mind the signals that are being sent with your present tense storytelling. As a leader, use storytelling to make your point, not argument.

Stories about the future are visions. To build a story like this, build it on something happening in the present, and project it into the future.

It is absolutely essential for leaders to engage in storytelling during the middle phase of an OAA Chapter of learning. For more guidance on how to use narrative and storytelling, examine the Bibliography and Resources sections found in the back of this handbook.

Handling Situations with Stories, not Sanctions

Various situations come up during a move to Agile. One situation that comes up frequently is "resistance". You might as well accept the idea that three to five percent of the people in your organization are probably Resistors. In an Agile adoption, the people fall into three broad categories. *Resistors* oppose the change. *Tolerators* have a wait-and-see, non-committal attitude. *Supporters* actively embrace the change.

If leaders tell stories about small successes with Agile during the middle phase, those who are resistant will either reform their behavior and become tolerant, or be repelled by what is going on and leave. Telling stories about the past, present and future of Agile in the organization is the way to address resistance. The exactly wrong thing to do is make a demand on a Resistor that they "get on board" or "get on the same page" as everyone else. Why? The reason is simple. A Resistor who feels forced is going to tell stories about being forced. These stories are very bad for your "open" Agile adoption. Therefore, it is a far better idea to tell stories every week... stories about:

- Any and all small successes with Agile inside the teams

- How the future looks (future tense stories, or visions)

- In general, how roles are changing and will continue to change, and how people are valued beyond the role they currently occupy

- How the organization is solving complex problems by being more open and encouraging much more experimentation (play)

Experimentation and Play

Leaders in the early going can do well by encouraging experimentation and play. As I said before, "experimentation" is the sanitized word for play. You might as well know right now that play is the name of the game. If your people are comfortable enough to play with various Agile techniques, you can expect good results. If however they feel compelled or otherwise forced to do these Agile practices, you can expect a problem. Always emphasize the importance of play in the beginning. If the word "play" is a censored word in your organization, use the word "experimentation". In either case, be sure to signal early and often your strong support for experimentation. Keep in mind that in Open Agile Adoption, this support for experimentation is essential. The emphasis on experimentation and play signals and confirms that these Agile practices are not mandated, and that the teams are figuring it all out. The emphasis on experimentation and play in your communications and storytelling cannot be overstated.

Teams Watch & Wait for Signals

Storytelling is a form of signaling. If leaders do not engage in storytelling, you can reasonable expect people to start to revert back to the old ways of working and being. Be sure to tell stories throughout the middle period of a Chapter of OAA learning. If you do not tell stories, the frequency and quality of your signals will be low, and you can definitely expect problems. Followers watch leaders for signals and signs. Stories are clear and strong signals that people can grab a hold of and use to navigate the changing landscape. Signal early and often. Tell stories in your own words about the past, the present and the future of the move to more Agile ways of working.

Storytelling on the part of leadership is an absolutely essential aspect of the Open Agile Adoption technique. If you are new to this idea take a look at the Bibliography and examine the titles related to storytelling.

Regarding Managers and Systems Architects

Managers often have trouble with Agile, because they hear that teams are self-managing...and these managers wonder what Agile means for their job. System architects also have trouble, because their status changes when Agile teams get formed. In both situations, you can get some resistance. Other team members may complain about others who are not playing the game. The answer to all of this is to tell stories.

Specifically, tell stories about:

- How people in management positions are valued, even if their old management roles are not

- How systems architects are valued

- In general, how roles are changing and will continue to change, and how people are valued beyond the role they currently occupy

- How the organization is solving complex problems by being more open and encouraging much more experimentation (play)

In general, the idea that people are more valuable than the roles they currently occupy is an important idea. The move to Agile is, in theory at least, a response to changing and challenging business conditions. In general, organizations are slow to create new roles that better serve the situation at hand. Further, and more to the point, if your organization sends the signal that roles are more important than the people who occupy them, you can expect trouble when you introduce Agile. You can expect people to revert back to the way things were, because that's the safe thing to do.

Signaling by leadership is the way out of this problem. In your storytelling and communications, be sure to send the signal that people are more valuable than the roles they currently occupy. Do your best to make people comfortable with changing roles frequently. In particular, try to assure managers and systems architects that they are valued and have a secure place in the new situation.

Notes on Ending in Open Space

OAA creates a containing structure for experiencing an Agile adoption in small yet significant stages. Each defined segment or stage begins and ends with an Open Space meeting. The ending is a big deal, and must be structured to deliver a sense of progress.

Leveling Up

The feeling of "leveling up" is essential. This statement is based on the hypothesis that people experience happiness when they experience a sense of progress. OAA is designed to deliver this sense of progress and accomplishment. The primary tool is the ending Open Space meeting. Before this meeting we tell stories about what is happening. During the meeting, we deliver a sense of progress. We do this in two ways: by having the ending meeting, and changing the authorized tasks of the person in the Coach role. After the meeting, the situation has changed. There is a change of state. There is a "leveling up".

New Facilitator Required

At the ending Open Space, a new Facilitator is a good idea. Having a new Facilitator makes the ending Open Space event different and unique, making the meeting distinctive. Having a new Facilitator also signals that the Coach's role is changing. The Coach may have facilitated the beginning Open Space and is not facilitating now.

Coach's Role Changes

At the beginning Open Space, we announced the specific way that the role of Coach would change. If the Coach was actively coaching practices, then this might change. If the coach was facilitating meetings, this pattern may end, and someone from inside the organization may assume this task. If the coach has been working with teams for several months, perhaps the change includes working just with facilitator and product people, or just with executive leadership. In any and all cases in OAA, it is essential that two things happen as part of every ending Open Space:

- The group is reminded of the specific and new and important changes in the Coach role

- The Coach and Sponsor work together to make sure this status change is fully operationalized going forward into the next Chapter

This is an essential aspect of the OAA approach. The authorized tasks of the Coach must change in a clearly announced and formal way during the ending Open Space. A good way to do this is for the Sponsor to specifically mention the change in Coach status during the opening of the meeting. Another good idea is for someone to convene a small session on a topic such as "Do We Need More Coaching?" or "What Does it Mean to Be Responsible for Our Own Learning?"

The Next Chapter

The ending Open Space also serves as the start of a new OAA Chapter. This needs to be reflected in the theme and related invitation. The ending Open Space is a termination and ending point for the previous Chapter, and the start of a new Chapter. Each organization will be unique, and have unique characteristics. The typical pattern is to have three Open Space events about 12 to 16 weeks apart. This provides two OAA Chapters of learning (essentially, structured passage rites) and sets the stage for incorporating periodic and recurring Open Space events on the calendar in July and January. The maturity of your organization in Agile terms will guide you on the question of whether to do one or two OAA Chapters of learning at the start

Making Open Agile Adoption a Part of the Culture

After the initial experience of using OAA to implement your Agile adoption, the final step is to place recurring Open Space events on the cultural calendar of the organization. The following advantages are gained by doing this:

- Creates ongoing safety to experiment

- Serves to initiate new hires

- Allows enough advance notice for everyone to plan to be there

- Installs Open Agile Adoption into the culture.

OPEN AGILE ADOPTION IN PRACTICE   47

- Removes dependency on any one formally authorized leader
- Provides an ongoing and clearly understood container for work

Let's examine each of these advantages in turn:

Creates ongoing safety to experiment

Just like at the start, the recurring Open Space meeting provides a venue for people to get together and tell the truth as they understand it. This has a very therapeutic effect on the members of your organization. They have a clear idea of when the next big opportunity is to review the experience just past, make adjustments, "call bullshit", and so on. Knowing that you are getting a hearing twice a year means that you can suspend your disbelief until that next meeting. Knowing the next meeting is coming also encourages the taking of careful notes that can be used for creating session ideas inside the Open Space.

Serves to initiate new hires

New hires get initiated into the culture of the place. Part social gathering, part serious business, and definitely fun, the Open Space meeting format is unique. New hires get told stories of previous Open Space events, and are encouraged to learn about it. A recurring Open Space event is a social event on the cultural calendar that new hires can use to make sense of the organization.

Allows enough advance notice for everyone to plan to be there

By having the recurring events on a definite schedule, with plenty of advance notice, everyone can be there. Leaders can show the way by avoiding any travel on that date, and encouraging other leaders to do the same. In this manner the recurring Open Space events become anticipated and serve the organization by breathing new life into it.

Installs Open Agile Adoption into the culture

By scheduling a recurring Open Space meeting, the cultural value of openness is made manifest. The very fact that the people in charge are authorizing such a meeting makes openness very real. Periodic Open Space events serve as a time of renewal and remembering, and signal to everyone that the openness value is very alive, and doing well.

Removes dependency on any one formally authorized leader

By getting policy established for two Open Space meetings per year, two big things happen. Open Space becomes woven into the cultural fabric of the organization, and the spirit of Agile and Open Agile Adoption does not go out the door when the progressive leader who started the process exits the company. This is a huge advantage for the organization that is using Open Agile Adoption. It removes any dependency on any one person and makes it possible to continue the Agile adoption story without them. Many Agile adoptions fail when the person who led the charge left the company. Open Agile Adoption places responsibility for Agile success with the people who do the work.

Provides an ongoing and clearly understood container for work

This is perhaps the biggest advantage of Open Agile Adoption: it creates a container for work. The container is created by boundaries, in this case a time boundary of six months duration. When everyone knows the boundary, they can and will adjust and self-organize around the known boundary. They will anticipate the next Open Space event, secure in the knowledge that Open Space is going to happen again, and that everyone is going to get a chance to speak candidly about what is working, what is not working, and what we might want to change.

OPEN AGILE ADOPTION IN PRACTICE

After About Two Years

Everybody knows that Agile change does not happen overnight.

Indeed, stories abound regarding how organizations spends millions of dollars trying to make a move to Agile, only to find that the organization reverts back to the old story after a brief delay.

What gives here?

The basic problem is that the members of the organization are not being invited but instead are being told to "be Agile", told to "do Agile", told to use Agile practices. We know that this does not produce a rapid and lasting Agile adoption.

What *does* work is *invitation*. And what is the essence of invitation?

I asked exactly this question on Twitter, and here are some of the responses I received:

"What is the essence of invitation?"

- Feeling welcome
- To offer the best you have without reservation
- To hold space for the possibility of fellowship
- Essence of invite is to incite...
- Questioning
- Inclusion
- Connection
- Bringing together groups with similar interests
- Free food
- An opening

- Mutual interests

- Friendliness

- Having fun with your friends

- Friendship

- The implied trust put in you by the inviter

As you can see, the essence of invitation is a key to success with your Agile adoption.

This is how it can be:

After about two years or so after you start with Open Agile Adoption, there will be Proceedings documents from at least three Open Space events. Conversations happened. People got introduced to each other, people that might have worked in the organization in some way for years and knew of each other, but never actually met.

Pictures got taken. Sessions got convened, discussions took place. There was some laughter and more than a little serious play... all under the cover story of "working together".

Proceedings were created, and some of the pictures that got taken of various folks attending, by various folks attending, made it into those proceedings. And those proceeding became cultural artifacts, created and actively used by the organization.

And as a result of those events, new ways of doing things emerged. Better ways. And some interesting stories began to be told.

And the people began to tell the tale of these new ways, and how the great and new ideas continue to be created...to this day...in the open space.

***

APPENDIX A

SELECTED BIBLIOGRAPHY

Note: By far the most important book in this list is *SPIRIT: Development and Transformation in Organizations*, by Harrison Owen. You can obtain it for free here: http://www.openspaceworld.com/Spirit.pdf

Bion, W. R. (1961). *Experiences in Groups: and Other Papers*. London, UK: Tavistock Publications. [Print].

Booth, S. L., & Meadows, D. L. (2010). *The Systems Thinking Playbook: Exercises to Stretch and Build Learning and Systems Thinking Capabilities*. White River Junction, VT: Chelsea Green Publications. [Print].

Cockburn, A. (2007). *Agile Software Development: The Cooperative Game.* (2nd ed.). Upper Saddle River, NJ: Addison-Wesley. [Print].

Csikszentmihalyi, M. (1990). *Flow: The Psychology of Optimal Experience*. New York, NY, USA: Harper & Row. [Print].

Denning, S. *The Leader's Guide to Storytelling: Mastering the Art and Discipline of Business Narrative*. USA: Jossey Bass. [Print].

Gharajedaghi, J. (2006). *Systems Thinking: Managing Chaos and Complexity: a Platform for Designing Business Architecture*. (2nd ed.). Amsterdam, NL: Elsevier. [Print].

Godin, S. (2008). *Tribes: We need you to lead us*. New York: Portfolio. [Print].

Hsieh, T. (2010). *Delivering Happiness: a Path to Profits, Passion, and Purpose*. New York: Business Plus. [Print].

Kline, P., & Saunders, B. (1998). *Ten Steps to a Learning Organization*. (2nd ed.). Arlington, VA: Great Ocean. [Print].

Logan, D., King, J. P., & Fischer-Wright, H. (2008). *Tribal Leadership: Leveraging Natural Groups to Build a Thriving Organization*. New York: Collins. [Print].

Margolis, M. (2009). *Believe Me: Why Your Vision, Brand, and Leadership Need a Bigger Story*. New York: Get Storied. [Print].

May, Matthew E. (2009). *In Pursuit of Elegance: Why the Best Ideas Have Something Missing*. New York: Broadway. [Print].

May, M. E. (2011). *The Shibumi Strategy: a Powerful Way to Create Meaningful Change*. San Francisco, CA: Jossey-Bass. [Print].

McGonigal, J. (2011). *Reality Is Broken: Why Games Make Us Better and How They Can Change the World*. New York: Penguin. [Print].

Mezick, D. (2012) *The Culture Game: Tool for the Agile Manager.* USA. Freestanding Press. [Print].

Owen, H. (2008). *Open Space Technology: a User's Guide*. (3rd ed.). San Francisco, CA: Berrett-Koehler. [Print].

Owen, H. (1987). *Spirit: Transformation and Development in Organizations*. Potomac, MD: Abbott Publishing. [Print].

Owen, H. (2000). *The Power of Spirit: How Organizations Transform*. San Francisco: Berrett-Koehler. [Print].

Owen, H. (1999). *The Spirit of Leadership: Liberating the Leader in Each of Us.* San Francisco, CA: Berrett-Koehler. [Print].

Owen, H. (2008). *Wave Rider: Leadership for High Performance in a Self-organizing World*. San Francisco: Berrett-Koehler. [Print].

Senge, P. M. (1990). *The Fifth Discipline: the Art and Practice of the Learning Organization.* New York: Doubleday/Currency. [Print].

Thomas, D., & Brown, J. S. (2011). *A New Culture of Learning: Cultivating the Imagination for a World of Constant Change.* Lexington, KY: CreateSpace. [Print].

Turner, V., (2001) *From Ritual to Theatre: The Human Seriousness of Play*, PAJ Publications. [Print].

APPENDIX B

ABOUT THE AUTHOR

Daniel Mezick is a management consultant and the pioneer in the use of Open Space to enable rapid and lasting Agile adoptions. Daniel has either facilitated or convened dozens of public and private Open Space meeting events since 2008.

Daniel is an author and keynote speaker on teams, teamwork and organizational change. He is the author of *The Culture Game*, a book of 16 patterns of behavior derived from Agile that can quickly make your team much smarter. *The Culture Game* was the result of experience and research since 2008, coaching Agile teams.

The Culture Game is showing up in some interesting places, including a Top 4 medical school, where teaching professors are using it to radically redefine how medical education happens. You can learn more at www.TheCultureGame.com.

Daniel is an approved speaker inside the highly selective VISTAGE INTERNATIONAL, the largest association of CEOs in the world. He delivers keynote speeches and seminars at numerous conferences around the world, including the South By SouthWest conference, the Global Scrum Gathering conference and the annual Agile Alliance conference.

(continued on next page)

ABOUT THE AUTHOR

Daniel is available for delivery of onsite, tailored consulting and training in the Open Agile Adoption method.

Public classes are held periodically in New York, Connecticut and Massachusetts.

To learn more about training and consulting options, please visit:

www.OpenAgileAdoption.com

Coaches and consultants interested in becoming licensed trainers in the Open Agile Adoption method are encouraged to contact the author.

You can reach Daniel as follows:

Daniel Mezick
http://newtechusa.net
203 915 7248
dan@newtechusa.net

BLANK PAGE FOR NOTES

BLANK PAGE FOR NOTES

BLANK PAGE FOR NOTES